Interviews with

John Morton

and

John-Roger

Religious Scholars Interview the Travelers

Interviews with

John Morton

and

John-Roger

Religious Scholars Interview the Travelers

M

Mandeville Press
Los Angeles, California

Published by Mandeville Press
P.O. Box 513935
Los Angeles, California 90051-1935
e-mail: jrbooks@msia.org

Visit us on the Web at www.msia.org

Printed in the United States of America
ISBN 0-893020-01-0

CONTENTS

INTRODUCTION

After Jim Lewis completed his marvelous book about MSIA, *Seeking the Light,* we had some conversations about the benefits of independent religious scholars researching MSIA and writing about their conclusions in academic papers. I spoke to some other scholars about this as well and, by early 1998, a project began to form with scholars from various areas of religious studies, especially those related to new religious movements, studying the Movement. The scholars were looking at MSIA from different perspectives that ranged from the origins of MSIA to a comparison with Eastern traditions.

In September 1998, Gordon R. Melton, Massimo Introvigne, Constance Jones, and Michela Zonta presented papers on MSIA at the CESNUR (Center for Studies on New Religions) conference in Turin, Italy. The conference was attended by academics from around Europe and the United States. John Morton and Vincent Dupont were also there. John even fielded some impromptu questions from scholars at the end of the MSIA presentation. Later in the year, papers were also presented at the Society for the Scientific Study of Religion meeting in Montreal by two other scholars, John Saliba and Robert Ellwood. Most recently, at the CESNUR conference in Bryn Athyn, PA in June 1999, three more new papers were presented by James Santucci, Dell deChant and Constance Jones. The idea of putting the academic papers together into an independently published anthology is currently being pursued under the editorship of Constance Jones.

To support the anthology project, John-Roger and John Morton have been interviewed by several of the scholars to assist them with their specific research. The great thing has been that each new interviewer has had the advantage of reading the previous interviews and thus has been able to go deeper with their questions. It has been extremely interesting to be a "fly on the wall" at these interviews. Both J-R and John have shared things that I had never heard in the years of my involvement in MSIA.

After reading several of the interviews as they were being done, MSIA's President Paul Kaye commented that the interviews would make very interesting reading for MSIA students and he asked Stede Barber to edit the content into readable form to create this special book. Since several of the interviewers asked the same or very similar questions, the answers to these questions were combined by Stede during the editing process. The interviews were further edited into a rough chronological order to illustrate the development of MSIA, and the role that John-Roger and John have played in making the work, teachings and guidance of the Mystical Traveler available to those who seek Soul Transcendence into the heart of God.

The interviews took place in Los Angeles over the past year and a half. The most recent was done on May 6, 1999 and the oldest was January 28, 1998. The five interviewers were J. Gordon Melton, a senior scholar of new religious movements who has published many books, including the *Encyclopedia of American Religions;* John A. Saliba, S.J. from the University of Detroit Mercy who has also published several books and papers; Massimo Introvigne, who founded CESNUR and has one of the most informative web sites about new religious movements in Europe (www.cesnur.org); Lou Ann Trost, the director at the Center for Theology and the Natural Sciences who recently got her PhD. at the Graduate Theological Union at Berkeley (and who is also a pastor in the Lutheran Church); and Constance Jones, a sociologist who teaches at the California Institute of Integral Studies and who has developed curriculum in women's studies, sociology of religion, social science methodology, and Eastern teachings. As a Fulbright scholar to India in 1995-96, she taught at Banaras Hindu University and Vasanta College and conducted research at the Krishnamurti Study Centre.

Each scholar approached their interview with the theme of their study. Massimo Introvigne was focusing on MSIA's history and origins, while Lou Ann Trost was writing about MSIA's concept of God. John Saliba was researching MSIA's plurality with other religions. As a sociologist, Constance Jones is looking at MSIA's sociological profile. She is the one who prepared the survey of MSIA participants that was mailed to half of the active Discourse subscribers in the United States, as well as over 400 inactive subscribers, in the summer of 1998. In the most recent interview, Gordon Melton tied up various angles on MSIA's history, theology, and more detail on the backgrounds of John-Roger and John Morton. The interviews often had unexpected responses, like the time Gordon asked John Morton to talk a little about his background and John talked in detail for about twenty minutes, saying things that even J-R had never heard before.

In the back of this book there is also a wonderful bibliography prepared by Theresa Hocking who, along with her husband Guy, assisted Stede with the editing of the interview transcripts. We hope that you enjoy reading these interviews.

Mark Lurie
MSIA Staff

1

J-R's Story

Interviewer: Were you having psychic experiences in your childhood, seeing and knowing things that other people weren't seeing and weren't knowing?

J-R: I could see things around people, their aura and their energy field, though it wasn't consistent. I thought everybody did that until I described someone to my mother one day and she said, "That person didn't have that color on at all."

My aunt had come to see my mom, and when I saw her, I said, "Mom, here comes Aunt so and so. She's got this strange red outfit on. You should tell her to go change, it's ugly and it doesn't look good on her." I went to my room while she visited, and after she left, my Mom said, "She didn't have any red on at all." My mother and I got into a who's-seeing-what discussion, and it hit me that my mom wasn't seeing what I saw. I asked her why my Aunt was there, and she said, "She was looking for her husband. She's so mad at him, she'd kill him if she could find him." I knew right then that what I'd seen was the anger aura. Nobody told me, I just knew it. My Mom and Dad and I talked all this over, and that's when I realized that other people didn't see what I saw.

Interviewer: Is there anything else significant from your childhood that hinted at what was to come in your life?

J-R: I can access a lot of things spiritually, but I can't access my childhood and most of my past. And believe me, I've asked why. If I can do all this, why can't I do that? If I can do healings with other people, why can't I do it on myself? The answer I've come to is, "Because you don't have a tendency for humbleness to start with. To keep you in that humble place, you have to humble yourself and go to other people for advice, direction and healing." It has worked very well. Maybe I would have been humble anyway, but part of me goes, "I doubt it."

Interviewer: What effect did your experiences prior to 1963, when you awoke to the "John" consciousness, have on you?

2

J-R: I refer back to them, often, in discussing things with people. They're helpful in relationships. Spiritually? No effect. I come present, right here, right now, spiritually.

Interviewer: Your information about what happened after the hospital experience in 1963 was really interesting.

J-R: That's just for this level, so people can have something to understand. It really doesn't help them to understand the Mystical Traveler Consciousness spiritually; that comes about by experience.

Interviewer: When you had your main spiritual experience, was it unexpected and sudden, like St. Paul in Damascus?

J-R: No, there was a progression. On July 4, 1963, I was in a pretty serious car accident. I was really dizzy and I couldn't walk. That put me in the hospital for a week or so. Then around December first of '63, I started urinating blood. The car wreck had pulled my kidney loose and dislodged a kidney stone. I went into the hospital for surgery, and was told that I was unconscious for nine days afterwards, but that I would open my eyes and look around and talk to people.

My mother was there the whole time, just devoted. When I came to, I looked at her and said, "Who are you?"

She said, "Who are you?"

I remember this; the voice said, "John."

She said, "Okay. Is Roger in there?"

This voice said, "Yes. Would you like to speak to him?"

It was like, click-click, and there was Roger.

I said, "Mom, I'm fine. Everything's fine. How did the surgery go?"

She said, "Have I got stuff to tell you." She told me that I had been diagnosing people in the hospital and knowing who was dying. They would bring people's charts in and read me the name and age. I'd tell them what was wrong; they'd check it out and come back and say that I was accurate. I don't remember any of this.

Interviewer: In retrospect, would you say the hospital experience was a first contact with the Traveler Consciousness?

J-R: I'd say that was the turning point. I think this consciousness was around way back in childhood experiences.

Interviewer: When did you realize that this new consciousness was the Traveler?

4

J-R: I don't know. Fairly soon after the surgery, I went to see a woman who channeled a consciousness called "E.C."—eternal consciousness. She could also channel others, like your basic self, your high self. She and the man she worked with came up with the name, "John-Roger."

I wanted to know what had happened during the surgery. They said that the consciousness that came in was "John."

When I asked, "John who?" they brought the consciousness in through this woman and I recognized it instantly. When it talked, I could feel it inside of me, like a small vibration that stopped when this consciousness stopped talking. I thought that was phenomenal. I asked, "Who are you? What do you do? Why are we together?"

It answered, "John the Beloved."

I asked, "Which John the Beloved?"

The answer was, "That one you'll find out in time."

I asked, "If this is John, am I now John? Or am I Roger? Who am I in here?"

They said, "You're both." They spelled it out for me, John hyphen Roger, and it fit. That's how the name came about. I don't know if I've even told this to the people who work around me.

Interviewer: Was this John the Beloved consciousness another consciousness in you, or a previous incarnation, or something similar?

J-R: They told me that I was this consciousness before, and am still this consciousness, and that it was now a spiritual sign that would be taking the lead of my spiritual path, my purpose. I don't remember the exact words, but the ideas are accurate. I've since found out that it was the one at the time of Jesus.

Interviewer: At that time, did you understand this presence of John the Beloved as what is now called the "Traveler Consciousness?"

J-R: No.

Interviewer: The messiah, or something different?

J-R: I had no idea what it was. I got out of the hospital on December 23rd, 1963. Then I spent two years, more or less, going around to various groups to check this, because I thought it was crazy. But I also had to entertain the idea that maybe it wasn't crazy.

Interviewer: Before your big spiritual experience in 1963, did you regard yourself as deeply religious, or not religious at all?

J-R: Spiritual. I didn't follow a doctrine. I researched a lot. I was looking for the upper. I laughingly refer to it as the time of my mental-physics and my being a meta-fizzle.

At one point, I went to the School of Christian Metaphysics where information from the Spirit world was coming through this man who did things you'd have to have seen to believe. You'd write a billet and drop it in a little wicker basket. He would tape silver dollars or fifty cent pieces over his eyes, and then tape cotton over his eyes. There was no way he could see. Then he'd tie a bandana around his head.

He would pick up one of those little billets, hold it and then call out your name. You'd say, "Here," and he would say, "The Spirit says this is what you want to know." I read those billets later, and sure enough—he was answering people's questions.

After about the second time of watching, I decided to have the experience for myself. I put my question into the basket, and when he pulled it out, he just nailed me right to the cross, bang, bang, bang. He answered things that I hadn't even put on there.

Another time, I went to see the man who wrote *Telephone Between the Worlds*. I was sitting a couple rows from the rear, and he said, "The young man in the back, with the lights all around you." It took me a couple minutes to realize that it was me he was talking about.

He had me come up front. He had a rod, and he held one end and had me hold the other end. I guess that was the "telephone." He said some really interesting things to me. At the time I was startled and in disbelief, but at the same time, I knew he was telling me the truth. By the time I got back to my seat, he'd left the stage and people were swarming around me, saying, "Did you hear what he said?" Everybody was wanting to touch me, they were literally falling on me and it took me awhile to get out of there.

Interviewer: Did you go back?

J-R: Once or twice. He said, "Just general encouragement—you're on a high path, it will be difficult at times, but always take courage, because God has done this."

Interviewer: Were other people having this kind of experience with you?

J-R: I went to hear Noel Street one time, and was sitting in the back of the room, as usual, so I could see what was going on. There were maybe forty of us in the room and he said, "The fellow on the very end of the row, with all the Lights dancing around him." We were all looking around to see who this could be. He finally narrowed it down to me. He had me stand up, and just said the nicest things. I was totally embarrassed, thinking, "You're seeing things way beyond what I see."

He did a reading on me the next day that blew me right out of the water. That was a sacred, holy time for me. I thought that if even a tenth of that came true, that would be a miracle. He was a big turning point with me.

Around 1970 or so, I took off for a month and just drove across the United States. I had to get away from it all and re-look at a lot of strange experiences. Those were turning points in my spiritual progression.

I wasn't having a hard time in my life, except for the first two years after the operation. I would see through things, like that wall, and would walk right into it, which seems kind of humorous now, although it wasn't at the time.

Interviewer: Did you start realizing what it was all about at that stage?

J-R: I don't know if I realize what it's all about right now. Pauli McGarry, who is now Pauli Sanderson, was great encouragement to me in those early years. I was doing seminars in Santa Barbara. During a seminar, my consciousness would alter and I would have all this information; then it would alter back. I didn't remember any of it, and Pauli would feed back to me what I had said, and what people had told her they had experienced. This played an important part in my awareness of what was going on.

Interviewer: Did you have any idea that there had been Travelers before you?

J-R: Not by that name. I knew I was connected to various people back through history. I would leave the body into the Spirit and track it back very precisely. Getting that information down through my mind so it would make sense on paper or a tape recorder was extremely difficult, however.

Interviewer: Was talking about the previous Travelers part of your first seminars?

J-R: No. I think the first seminars and Light studies were establishing the validity of this "John" consciousness, and that it did, indeed, know what it knew.

Interviewer: Were you doing seminars for twenty or so people before you started working with people on a one-to-one basis?

J-R: Some of that was happening at the same time. "Light Studies" were the one-on-one sessions.

Interviewer: What was the nature of the Light studies?

J-R: Past life, mostly; looking at what people were doing that wasn't working and tracking it to a source. When I hit on something, I could see the Light picking it up and off. I would see a person's lifetimes like a fan of cards or a reel of something around their head. I would tell them what I saw and how that was playing out in their life. People would often say, "Oh my God! How could you know that?" I didn't know it; I told them what I saw, and their job was to sort out what worked and what didn't.

I looked at what I was doing as "Spiritcology," like spiritual psychology. Some people were having six or seven Light studies because releasing them from one bondage allowed the bondage underneath that to start surfacing. That was a unique experience for me.

We eventually reached a point where a lot of what was showing up was typical of being human, and I started doing seminars that were really Light studies for everyone in the room.

Interviewer: What were the dynamics of the seminars, and your schedule at that time?

J-R: I taught high school until December 17, 1971 and was also doing seminars five or six nights a week and Light studies during the week and all day Saturday and Sunday. I'd do a Light study or two after school, then drive to the seminar location, which was often a two-hour drive. Then the seminar would be two to four hours long, and I'd drive back home. I used to get home around midnight, one o'clock and was back up again at 6:00 a.m. getting ready for school and reviewing what I was going to do for the day. That was pretty much the routine.

During the seminar, I would pick up each person in the room and work with their consciousness, which is why the tapes all have rambling information on them. People would often say, "At one point he spoke directly to me and what I'm dealing with, but I don't get this other part." Somebody else would say, "That part was mine."

We started tape recording the seminars and people were sending tapes to friends and family all over the country. We started being asked to go to other locations where there were forty or fifty people lined up for Light studies. We were also doing polarity balances, aura balances, innerphasings, and open seminars.

If you had asked us where this was going, we'd have said, "Just follow along and take notes; we'll know at the end." There was no real goal out there. I'd really have to call it fate.

Interviewer: You started doing seminars in 1965; when was MSIA was incorporated?

Mark Lurie: MSIA was officially incorporated in 1971.

Interviewer: How did the name MSIA come about?

J-R: We were at someone's home to do a seminar and a woman told me that her husband wanted to come, but first he wanted to know what we were called.

I told her that we weren't called anything. We were moving our spiritual inner awareness to a greater awareness.

She said, "Moving, Movement of Spiritual Inner Awareness?" She picked up on my description and named it. And her husband showed up the next week.

Interviewer: Were people who attended seminars associated with other religious groups? Were they people who had tried different things, like Scientology one day, EST another day, and then MSIA?

J-R: In those early days, I'd say they all came out of a Christian background. Some people had studied with other groups. I never really asked, because the less I knew about them personally, the more effective I was in giving information. I had no concern about hurting feelings; I focused on dealing in truth as much as possible.

2

John's Story

Interviewer: What was your background, John? Were you a member of any church before MSIA? Or a religious person?

John Morton: No. My family went to Lutheran Church occasionally, not very often, and I never went through any formal catechism or anything like that. My brother and sister did. I wasn't really interested at a young age.

Interviewer: Could you briefly share about your career in MSIA? How long you've been in, how you got started and that kind of thing?

John Morton: I never really thought of it as a career, but that's good. It's getting up in the amount of time that it must be a career. Around 1970 or so, I started picking up an interest in inner kinds of things. Philosophy, meditation; I started reading some general things, and took some courses at the University of California at Davis.

I took a class from Charles Tart, who is fairly well known in parapsychology. In his class we read *The Teachings of Don Juan, The Master Game,* and we read about alternative religions. We read a series of books that, to me, opened up all kinds of things. When I started reading *The Teachings of Don Juan,* I began to realize that I was looking for a teacher.

I was reading a big manual about parapsychology, *Altered States of Consciousness* by Charles Tart, while I had him as a professor. He was very much into Carlos Castaneda. He had been in contact with Carlos Castaneda and he played an interview with him that he had done for the class. I guess that was pretty rare at the time, because Castaneda was very reclusive.

That kind of ignited things. We studied a book on new religions which talked about various things going on. It was a very active period and I was reading about all kinds of things.

I came closest to being involved with Elizabeth Claire Prophet. They had a gathering in Shasta, I think it was in 1975. By that time I had been to one MSIA seminar the year before. I'd met someone in Sacramento, where I was going to school, who was doing home seminars, playing John-Roger audio tapes. I wasn't even on Discourses at that point. Then I heard about this event up in Shasta and I went up there. They do the "fiats," and they do rhythmic chanting. Elizabeth Claire Prophet was, I would call it channeling, these ascended Masters. That's what she was claiming.

J-R: Was that after her husband died?

John Morton: Yes. I remember that at one point, she had one called K-12 or something like that; it didn't have a name. Almost the entire audience went unconscious, including a friend of mine who started kind of babbling. I thought, "This is pretty interesting." What I noticed was that up in Mt. Shasta, where it was a warm day but not hot, there was this radiant heat that came through us, like a wave. I started looking around and noticing some people were "out." It seemed like there were only one or two people who were still up, and I was one of them, just listening to what she was saying. Then my friend got spooked and wanted to leave. He had some very powerful experience, like a rebirthing, and it rattled him. I was mostly just interested; I'd never been to something like that.

I had some very interesting experiences that were paranormal, or metaphysical. It was obviously quite powerful. I was having inner experiences and yet it still was not what I was looking for. That was an interesting experience in and of itself. I thought, "There must be something, because I'm on to something that's at least having a powerful impact."

At that time, I was starting to get information from "Summit Lighthouse," I think that's what they called it. I read about Edgar Cayce, and thought that was interesting. I read the *Seth Speaks* material by Jane Roberts. Her stuff was interesting, but for me it was, "No, I'm not interested in that either."

What I became interested in was having some answers. Maybe I was one of the so called, "seekers." I didn't formally join any group. I did go into some situations. I went to an introduction for Transcendental Meditation, and I had a pretty neutral response. It just didn't particularly interest me at the time. A couple of people talked to me about Scientology, also.

In 1974 when I was a Park Ranger, I talked to another Park Ranger to catch up, and he mentioned going to spiritual awareness seminars. I asked him about that, and he said, "There's one in someone's home," which caught my interest. I went to one and they did a HU chant, which is fairly typical if you go to a home seminar. They call in the Light and they do some chanting. I remember it was "H-U," and I had a very powerful experience with it. I was sitting on a couch wondering, "What is this?" I hadn't done chanting, and at that point in my readings, I was aware that you can invoke all kinds of things. I wondered, what am I invoking here? I had a sense that it was okay, that the energy in this group was fine. But as soon as I uttered that sound out loud, I had a very powerful experience, as if I was going up in a rocket ship at light-speed. It was so physical in nature that I hunched down because I thought I was going to hit the ceiling. I repeated this at least four times before I could get over the reaction and just chant with this rush of energy. What do you do with something like that? There's not too much you can do because it's an experience, it's not really explained. There's no narration. I wasn't hearing a voice or something like that. It was just a very powerful experience.

Then I listened to the seminar tape, which was on a relatively crude cassette machine that somebody put in the middle of the room. It was hard to hear, and I think it was a poor quality recording. I don't think we had anywhere near the technology we do now. Plus, J-R's style doesn't necessarily follow a straight line. It's not like, first you say what you're going to say, then you say it, then you tell everybody what you said. It wasn't anything like that. So I didn't relate to what was said, but I had a powerful experience.

I remember reading one of the pamphlets that was there, and having a strong experience with the information. What it was saying resonated with what I was looking for.

I didn't really get more involved until a year later. The person who was holding the seminars was a student and it was the end of the school year, so the seminars stopped for the summer. Then I changed jobs and decided to go back to school in the fall. I had the information in a box that I didn't unpack, and months went by. In the back of my mind, I had the idea that I would contact that group and see what it was about, but no one contacted me and I don't think I was on any kind of mailing list. I just had a little pamphlet at that point.

In the spring, I had a job in a children's receiving home. One of my co-workers mentioned she was going to a Wesak Festival. I remember asking, "What's a Wesak Festival?" She told me it was an annual celebration of Buddha, and that there would probably be some meditation. I went, and it was nice. She introduced me to her neighbor who was wearing a lapel pin that really got my attention. It was an MSIA logo about the size of a nickel. I remember reading the words out loud, "Movement of Spiritual Inner Awareness," and thinking, "Hey, is that this group?"

I said, "I've been looking for this group, I've been thinking I wanted to contact them." I couldn't remember John-Roger's name. I said, "I think there's a guru," and she said, "No, there's no guru."

I said, "Are you sure? Isn't there somebody who's the leader?"

She said, "Not really. But there's somebody who gives talks."

I said, "Is it a man named Rogers or something like that?"

And she kept saying, "No."

I said, "Well, who is it?"

She said, "There's a John-Roger."

I said, "That's it!" One thing led to another and she mentioned that she was holding seminars in her home, that she'd just started, and there was just her and one other person in Sacramento. I remember considering the odds of that—there were at least half a million people in Sacramento back then, moving towards a million. Given the odds of running into the one person who was involved in MSIA, I found it interesting that I found that person.

I started attending home seminars on a regular basis; that was in 1975. I started reading Discourses and got some aura balances, and started studying towards initiation. In 1977, I got my causal initiation. During that period, I found that I was having the experiences that were being talked about in the Discourses and seminars.

At the same time, I was getting my Master's degree in counseling and I got married in January of 1977. I was developing that track—getting married, getting my Master's degree, looking at going into counseling as a profession, looking for where I was going to work and what field I was going to go into and all those things. In there somewhere, I thought about spiritual counseling. In researching what specialties and programs were out there, I never ran across a program in spiritual counseling. About the closest thing was being a chaplain, because that tended to be non-denominational. My personal view on the counseling and psychology field was that it was almost anti-God. God was virtually a taboo subject in therapy. I thought that was odd, because psychologically, most people seem to have God in their beliefs and some of their confusion was with God and trying to sort out why God would do things in certain ways. I thought, "Well, it seems to me that it might be valuable to open up a field, a counseling specialization, that was called spiritual counseling or psychology. If someone was trying to sort out the God part of everything, I thought that there might be a way of relating to that person.

Around that time, I started having inner visions. Maybe they were dreams, maybe they were just images.

One of them that I kept seeing was me up in front of large groups of people wearing a suit, teaching, but more like preaching. There wasn't a pulpit and there wasn't a Bible. I didn't know what that was. I didn't even own a suit at that point. Then I got a job as an employment counselor with an employment agency; they required that I wear a coat and tie. I thought, "Maybe that's it." But that didn't seem to be the experience.

I was graduating in June of 1978, which was the first year of Insight. Two women in Sacramento were the main people in MSIA there besides me. One of them took Insight and she thought it was the best thing that ever happened. She kept telling us about it, and she kept saying, "You really should do this. This is a really great program." She'd say, "You know, John-Roger is involved."

My thinking was, "Well, I've just been through four years of counseling, group therapy and group facilitation training, and I have probably seen almost all of what this is. I don't know what it is, but I've been doing it."

In June/July 1978, there was an MSIA Conference with a retreat, an Initiates' Meeting and an Insight Seminar. I decided that I'd go do the MSIA Retreat at Lake Arrowhead, the Insight I seminar and then attend the Initiates Meeting. There was a guest event for Insight the Monday prior to when the

Insight I was starting, and I went to it. I walked into the room and as soon as I saw the facilitator up front, it was déja vu, this is what I'd been seeing in my visions; everything was there except me up in front.

That was one of those spine-tingling experiences. I thought, "Wow, this is it." And Insight was really a wonderful experience, there's no question about it. At Conference that year, John-Roger was talking about all kinds of things that were going to happen with Golden Age Education, things that I think related to what the University of Santa Monica has become as well as Peace Theological Seminary, The Institute for Individual and World Peace, and the Heartfelt Foundation. The University was not in existence at that point. J-R talked a lot about education and transformation, how that work was going to be done through what he was doing, and that a lot of other people were going to get involved. I just knew he was talking to me at that point. Maybe he was talking to everybody, but I felt the message was directly to me, like a call, "We're going to do this. People are going to be involved, there's a lot of work to do." I felt like, "I'm the one, I'm somebody who's going to do that."

Around that time, I wrote a letter to John-Roger, care of the MSIA office, something very general like "I'd be interested in working, I just graduated from Insight I and if there's any opportunity," etc. I received a letter back from the MSIA office letting me know that my intention to do the work that J-R was doing was nice and that I should look at general ways of supporting it. I interpreted this response as, "Thanks but no thanks."

There was a service seminar that year in two parts, and there were a couple of retreats at Lake Arrowhead that I attended. MSIA was progressively becoming more powerful for me, and it started putting tension into my marriage at that time. My ex-wife was okay with MSIA, but she was basically a devout Catholic. To a certain degree, she was interested and open to what we did, but she was starting to get angry. She felt I was being pulled into MSIA and she was asking, "What about our plans?" We had a counseling therapy career track that we were going to do together, et cetera, but it seemed like I wanted to work for this group which was in Los Angeles, and she didn't want to go to there, etc.

So, that factor with my ex-wife and the impact of MSIA was building. It caused so much tension at one point that she said, "I need to go spend some time alone and think; I'm going to my parents for awhile. I don't want to be in contact, so don't call me." She left. Then about three days later, she called me. I think the very first words out of her mouth were, "I know who John-Roger is."

I said, "What do you mean?"

25

She said, "I don't want to talk about it," but she proceeded to say, "I understand now why you want to go work for him. I'll support you, I'll help you financially. If you want to get divorced, I understand."

I was surprised to say the least. We'd previously had all this tension and arguing about MSIA, and now she'd made a one hundred and eighty degree change: totally supportive, letting me go, letting me be free in whatever choice I elected. In her own way, she was a tuned in person; she would see nature spirits and devas and this was a very private, personal world that she hardly talked about to anyone. She told me that she'd had a visit from John-Roger. I realized that she didn't mean he'd come to her house. It was so personal to her that she didn't want to go into detail. She said, "All I'll say is, I know who he is and I understand why you're interested and why it's so important to you."

That seemed to smooth out a lot of our tension, and at that point, I thought that we could work something out with our marriage that included involvement with MSIA. I thought that since she now knew who J-R was, maybe she would get more involved and it would be perfect.

She did come to an MSIA retreat at Lake Arrowhead in August, 1978. She also got her own apartment around this time. I ended up moving out of the house in which we had resided and into the apartment with her. As soon as I did that, the tension between us started building all over again. Everything had opened up so that I could go and do whatever I was doing with MSIA, including move to Los Angeles. When I chose not to do that immediately, everything started falling apart again.

Around that time the same friend who had done Insight I was now doing Insight II and was really encouraging me to do it also. Her graduation was during the very retreat at Lake Arrowhead that my ex-wife attended. I changed my plans to attend my friend's Insight II graduation while my ex-wife elected to return to Sacramento.

That was a powerful experience in and of itself. I'd never seen my MSIA friend so lit up, totally bright, happy, joyful. The graduates were sharing in a similarly amazing way and I decided, "I have got to go do that." I knew I wanted whatever had them all lit up, each in their own way, so I enrolled in Insight II.

My ex-wife was bothered by that decision and I decided that I would make my decision about going to be involved in John-Roger's work at my Insight II. I would either move and get involved, or I would just drop it and go on with my life, my marriage, my career, etc.

John-Roger was involved pretty much full time in that Insight II. The training was a completely transforming experience for me from the first moment. Everything shifted and changed, and what was abundantly clear was that I was going to get involved. Insight had a guideline that participants couldn't make any major changes for two weeks after the training because they knew people were flooded emotionally. If I was going to move, quit a job, leave a relationship, those kinds of things, then I needed to let things calm down first for at least two weeks. I waited and when those two weeks were up, I was in my car driving to Los Angeles. I knew that I was most likely getting out of the marriage, but we left that decision suspended.

I did not know where I was going to live, I did not know what I was going to do. I called my Insight II buddy and asked if I could stay with her. She said I could stay for one night because her mother was coming into town after that. So I had a place for one night.

The next morning I called the MSIA office and asked if there was a way I could meet with John-Roger. I told them that he'd done my ordination blessing and had said he'd be interested in listening back to the information some time. The response was something like, "You could send him the tape," but I told them no, I wanted to meet with him in person.

They explained that there were a lot of requests and they didn't know when or even if he would meet with me. That was fine with me, so they told me they'd get back to me when they knew something.

I said, "I'll be here."

Whoever I was talking to laughed and said, "It won't necessarily be today. It could be several days before I have a response."

I said, "Well, I really don't have anything else that I need to be doing, so I'll just be here."

About an hour later, she gave me a call and said that J-R could meet with me that day. I immediately went up to his home and met with him. We talked about all kinds of things that day. I think it was about six or seven hours later when he asked me if I was getting hungry. We went out to dinner and he asked me where I was staying that night. My car was out in the driveway and I said, "Well, right now the car's looking like it might be the place." He mentioned that there was a motor home that they had parked by the house; it didn't have electricity, etc. I said, "That's all right," and that's where I started, staying in the motor home up on the church property in Mandeville Canyon.

I started doing things like sweeping the driveway and raking leaves, cleaning, washing dishes and odd things like that. They would invite me to breakfast and then to lunch; it was a very casual thing. There was nothing like, "Would you like to stay? Would you like to work with us?"

During that initial six hour stint, J-R asked me something like, "What would you like to do?" I said I would like to get involved in what he was doing. I had this strange feeling that he was really asking me what I'd like to do if I had my wish or could have my heart's desire. In my own way, I hedged my bet and said I'd like to work with Insight. The reality was that I wanted to travel with J-R, go wherever he went and learn everything I possibly could learn about what he was doing and who he was. But I didn't say that.

When I said the thing about Insight, J-R picked up the phone and called the Insight office. He asked them when the next Insight seminar was and asked me what it was I wanted to do with Insight. I didn't know how to answer that question.

I said, "I just want to support it."

J-R said, "Support how?" I couldn't believe these questions. I wasn't used to being put in the position of being asked, what do you really want? I wasn't prepared to say what I wanted. There were two seminars coming up at simultaneous times. I asked J-R if he was going to be involved in them, and when he said yes, I told him, "I'd like to be involved in whatever and wherever you are."

He told the Insight office, "We'll have him float in between the two seminars." That's what they wrote in their log for the training: "John Morton, floater." People involved with Insight often wonder where that term came from; it's one of those little things in the annals of Insight lore.

I made a conscious decision at that point that even though I was raised to be polite and considerate, they were going to have to ask me to leave. I would stay in the motor home or I would do something. I think J-R was supportive of that part of it. I started being more and more involved. In January of 1979, there was a trip up to San Francisco where there was a workshop for Insight, and I was invited to go up there.

At that point, one of the long-time members of the staff who traveled with J-R was leaving, and I saw an opportunity there. The other staff were invited to talk to me and one or two other people about being part of the staff who traveled and worked closely with J-R. I was the one who was chosen.

I got involved with Insight, learning how to facilitate. Within about six weeks, I was up front with a suit on, fulfilling the vision that I'd seen. Of course, that vision also relates to the MSIA seminars and workshops I now do.

Within a short period of time, I became the Vice President of MSIA. I was amazed by that because in terms of seniority, I didn't have any. That's how it began. I don't know if that was too much for what you were asking.

Interviewer: No, it was exactly what I was looking for.

J-R: I was very interested. I didn't know a lot of this.

Interviewer: What was your experience at first of holding the keys to the Traveler consciousness?

John Morton: There were obviously things leading up to that period. Part of the keys were passed at the Initiates Meeting on June 19, 1988. Then more took place on December 18, 1988. I knew that some things were starting to shift. I noticed it in my interactions with people. I was doing ministerial services, aura balances, polarity balances, etc., but in my one-to-one contact with people, I noticed that information started presenting itself to tell people. I knew this was coming from a higher consciousness than what I was usually aware of. People would tell me, "What you just said was moving, or really powerful. I felt a blessing, the Spirit, the Traveler." When I did an ordination blessing, my experience was one of giving over, allowing myself to listen, and then speaking what I heard. Prior to the passing of the keys, there were a few of the ordinations where I would hear, "This Traveler." I would hesitate, thinking that I was not the Traveler. I would go ahead and say it and later think, "The Traveler is doing the blessing and I was just letting them hear the words from the Traveler; they may think I was talking about 'this Traveler, John Morton,' but I wasn't, really."

When the keys got passed, that experience was one of the little footnotes that I looked back on and thought, "There's Spirit, winking at me again, saying, 'I got you, now you're a Traveler, so when someone hears John Morton giving the blessing and saying, 'This Traveler,' they'll go, 'Yes, John was a Traveler.'" But I wasn't the Traveler at that point in terms of the keys.

J-R: Everyone's the Traveler in that big sense of the word. His just identified itself.

John Morton: As far as leading up to receiving the keys, there was a very brief conversation where J-R said something on the order of, "Are you willing to be the Traveler?" or "Are you willing to have the keys passed to you?" I don't recall the precise words, but that's how I have it inside. The way I related to that in my consciousness was service, that this was an extension of serving. If this in some way serves, then yes. I didn't know what it meant, and I didn't stop and say, "Okay, but can you tell me what the changes are and what's going to be required of me?" Inside of me, that didn't matter. There was no discussion. I just saw it as service, so I said, "Yes."

As I recall, it showed up when J-R went up on stage during the Initiates meeting. Inwardly, I just knew, "I think this is going to be the passing of the keys." I hadn't seen that before, and I hadn't seen it spiritually. I didn't know what was going to happen. J-R announced it from the stage; I think he looked at his watch and said the time. At some point, John-Roger invited me to say something. I went up on stage and what I recall saying was that it was just like breathing. That was how I was experiencing it. There was no conscious shift that I could tell you about. I just experienced it as subtle and yet as powerful as a breath of air, a light going on, an energy....

J-R: No, it happened many years before at Mandeville Canyon. You received an enlightenment. That's when all that took place. It was five to seven years later when it showed up physically. Do you understand what I'm talking about?

John Morton: I remember something very powerful that happened.

J-R: Up at Mandeville?

John Morton: I was sobbing and...

J-R: That's when it happened. That's when you totally looked up and said, "Yeah, I agree."

John Morton: OK. So I can relate to it in a linear fashion. It's more like, when does conception takes place? You can say, "When the sperm enters the egg," but when or where does that take place in a human consciousness? How do you relate to it from a consciousness standpoint? I don't know. It's pretty infinite or subtle.

I talked about how I saw that what I was doing, what I had been doing, was really supporting what John-Roger had already established: the teachings as a reference point. I saw that I was going to go off and do my ministry sooner or later and some would come with me and some would stay. It's pretty much been that ever since. I don't see any difference in what I'm to do, other than to extend what's already been done.

During those months, there was an awkwardness that I was dealing with. I don't remember when it stopped, or the last time it happened, because it has still happened on occasion. I've had several times where I've woken up and felt something like fear, but I don't think it's really fear. It's more of being startled, where you suddenly take in a breath. I was aware of the weight of the Traveler, of the burden and immensity of it. I was looking at the

Traveler Consciousness from a human flesh and blood standpoint, and wondering, what kind of authority do I have, what kind of abilities do I have, what kind of experience do I have? I feel very infinitesimal in relation to it. It's like the gap between who the Traveler is in Spirit and who the Traveler is in John Morton. It seems immense. I usually just get over it. I breathe in and realize that it's not about physical abilities or human abilities, it's about stepping up to the plate.

I've often related to people that what I do is show up. There are meeting places that are prepared, places that I have to go to physically. That's the Traveler's work in this world, to physically anchor and to physically be in a place and a time in a relationship of some kind. It sounds like it's very specific and detailed, but it has freedom. There's choice in it, but I find that, as a Traveler, there are certain things I have to do. Fortunately, I don't find that I'm resisting that on a personal level. There are times when I experience it as inconvenient or uncomfortable or something like that, but it's not really an issue. It's like getting up when you just don't feel like getting up. You know you've got to and you do.

I don't know at what stage of maturing or taking it on that I'm in, but I know that I'm in a maturing process. I'm aware that my ability to hold the consciousness is being increased, because that's what happens by holding the consciousness. You either increase, or it goes away. There's no choice that I know of in that process. The ability to just stand with it somehow increases by holding it.

I find that reflected back to me from time to time. Someone will write to me and essentially say, "I just got you as the Traveler for the first time," though they may have been involved in 1988. There are people who are still getting the connection. I look at that as natural because J-R is still working with them as their Traveler.

Just because I hold the keys doesn't necessarily mean that the Traveler Consciousness would go to them and say, "That's the Traveler." They're having a relationship with John-Roger; that's in Spirit and it's already in place. I'm not here to take that over. J-R's initiates are his initiates. But I have people who I work with.

J-R: The best way to say that is the Traveler through me has its initiates, and the Traveler through you has its initiates. John-Roger has no initiates. It's just the time period when the connections were made.

Interviewer: You are getting to my next question. Have some of the students who began working with you, J-R, before 1988, continued to work with you? Have some transferred and now work with John? And do the new initiates work with John?

J-R: No. Let's see, how do I say it so it doesn't make you wrong. They're all initiates of the Traveler. For awhile I was the one who stood forward and held the keys in the physical, and the people who were initiated during that time were the ones who I initiated. Then I moved back and John moved forward. I was never the physical Traveler for those people. I was always their spiritual Traveler, so that remains.

If I were to die, then they would go to John physically. The Traveler that's in him is the same one that's in me. That would just somehow shift and he would tie into the information and give it to them. Are they then John's initiate? No, they're always the Traveler's initiate. There's really no differentiation. But what am I doing?

I'm trying to give him more of everything that I used to do so I can do less. I'll do more and more of less and less until I do everything about nothing.

I hold one of the keys in the Spirit world, and the others are held by him in the physical. All the other Travelers in Spirit line up behind the one who anchors the physical to make sure that that one has the flow.

In other times in the Spirit worlds, Spirit didn't do that and there was falling apart and falling away.

We end up with sectarianism and denominational-ism throughout the planet because there was this type of thing going on. I think it's all part of the evolution of separation and coming back together again, so it's not bad.

Interviewer: Just one final concept. The concept of the keys. When I hear that, I immediately shift back to the book of Matthew about the keys of the kingdom, the authority. I assume that, since keys unlock things, they unlock the doors to the various levels and realms. Have I misinterpreted, or is that accurate?

J-R: Look at it more like the keys on a piano. How many songs can you play on the piano?

Interviewer: Infinite number.

J-R: That's infinite keys. It's harmonics. It's the sound. And the sound can be broken up into many, many different sub-sections.

Interviewer: John, how do you look at being the Mystical Traveler?

John Morton: I look at it as a willingness to choose to hold the consciousness. To walk with it like a job. That would be one way of looking at it.

One of the profound parts is that it doesn't necessitate that I be some kind of living master who is out doing miracles. That's not what was required. If that was required, then I wouldn't qualify. It just asked for a willingness, and then there is a state of cooperation. I don't think that if I was going out and killing and maiming and robbing and pillaging that I would be the Traveler, but that's my speculation. Maybe the next Traveler will prove me wrong.

So what is that? Well, it's not a respecter of persons, so it's not about what's happening here on the earth. It's about change and transition. I'm still someone who expresses the laws and the negativity of being human. I'm not perfect. Yet there is this consciousness that I have an awareness of and access to that entails that I partake. When someone is brought to me or is in some way making it clear that they're here for that, I'm on purpose.

Interviewer: So if I come to you and I say I'm wide open to, what, mingling our spirits, or energies, or whatever, would that be what you're talking about?

John Morton: No, it's not a personal thing. It's that I'm wide open to God, I'm wide open to who I am, I'm wide open to the truth, I'm wide open to love. I'm with you. That's the direction that the Traveler is going. The direction the Traveler is showing you is that it is unconditional love, unconditional acceptance. It's the truth, the living truth. That's the direction. Yet it is a consciousness that's in every level. It's just that its direction is a turning if that's what is necessary.

Interviewer: Do you feel more of an ability to do the kind of energy things I've seen J-R do?

John Morton: Yes, and part of it is getting up to the plate and taking a swing. How do I know I'm going to hit the ball? I don't. I don't know if anything is going to happen. If you were to ask, "How do you get this ability? Are there great masters guiding you? Are there voices or some energy? Or is it, you're just following?" I'd say that I follow intuition for the most part. If I see or hear something, I cooperate. I try to become as invisible as I can in the process of working with people. That's what I'm doing right now. I'm trying to make this as impersonal as I can, and yet it's personal. You're asking, what's my experience? What's my view? I can't divorce myself from that, and that's not what's called for here. That's why we say we don't do channeling. I'm not going out of my consciousness or getting out of the way and letting some other consciousness take over; that's not what's being done. Certainly there's an influence, so you say, "I experience the influence of this or that or someone." I've experienced great masters in J-R's presence, and seen them on his face.

Interviewer: How has that happened?

John Morton: It just appears. I remember one occasion where J-R asked, "What do you see, who do you see?" My answer was, "Lao Tsu." J-R asked me how I knew that. I saw someone and I didn't necessarily recognize them; I heard the name. J-R said, "How'd you do that?" I was listening. That's how simple it is. It isn't some great mystery or formula or anything like that. It's just being open.

I watch and do what J-R does all the time. Not literally all the time, but it's always available as a process. And it can be very different. I've been with him when he really has a very striking change of personality, the voice and everything. It's unusual. He's talked about dealing with someone, and he'll say, "That's your father you just heard." Unless you're really paying attention you wouldn't necessarily notice. His walk and posture and things like that will change. It isn't like he goes unconscious. I don't experience that kind of influence at this point, and I don't know that I will. It works with me how it works with me.

Mostly I see my job as showing up, and when it's clear to be in a place and a time, then I do that. I work carefully at it. I also still do all the things that any of us would do, from the mundane, ordinary standpoint. There are foods I like and foods I don't like, and people I like or I don't like, and all of those kinds of responses.

Sometimes J-R will do really outrageous things. If you want to see somebody do outrageous things, watch John-Roger. A lot of people don't like him. They think he's a phony, the biggest rip-off artist they've ever seen. I'm sure you've read it, it's around. I just see that as part of the test. When I listen from the heart, not just to what I see or hear, or just to what the mind presents, but from a heart-felt place, I find the Spirit is with me. I experience this presence as always with J-R and it conveys itself. It transcends his behavior, his mannerisms, what he says and things like that.

There are often two shows going on, and there's often a place where it all merges where he's a saint in the flesh. There are times when you wonder, how can this guy possibly pretend to know anything spiritual? You look at him and there's this range in the expression. That's one of the ways that people come into MSIA. Piety in the ritual sense is not something that we practice much of. It's almost like we'll do anything not to be ritualistic. I love that it's not about, "You have to dress like this, you have to eat this way, you have to behave this way," etc. It's about the spiritual directives of how you live your life.

3

Gems

Interviewer: What does MSIA teach about the relationship between God and the material world?

J-R: Let's look at this bottle as being empty. Then we blow some smoke into it and close off the top. When you look in the bottle, you'll see smoke, but it will be hard to see. If we could condense the smoke, we would come to the place where we wouldn't be able to see through the bottle because the smoke would be so dense. If we expanded the bottle, the smoke would be dissipated until you could hardly tell it was there; the bottle might look like an empty container. As we condensed it again, the smoke would once more become visible, and we would have something that looked very material.

We are just condensed Spirit. We're all Spirit and we're condensed into the material form. So the material form isn't looked at as alien or as separate from Spirit; it's really a continuum. There's no relationship between God and the material world, there is only a continuation of what is.

Interviewer: This relationship or continuum is where you talk about the Sound and Light as being central to our lives. Would you say that the Sound and Light come from God?

J-R: When we look at this table which has a glass top, we could say, "We see this because it is materializing according to our senses." We call that the magnetic light. Magnetic light is prevalent here in the material world as what we can perceive with our physical senses. We look at the Light of the Holy Spirit as the glass on top of the table. The glass can't be here without the table. The Holy Spirit rides on the magnetic light in this physical world. We see the manifestation of the Holy Spirit by how it performs through the magnetic light, which is in direct contact with people.

That magnetic light is what happens in the churches where someone touches another person and just knocks them down, or waves their arm and people fall. You are seeing the manifestation of the magnetic light. The Holy Spirit functions more through the Soul atmosphere. The magnetic light functions through the levels below the Soul: the physical, astral, causal, mental and etheric realms.

The Holy Spirit can ride the magnetic light into the lower levels, but the magnetic light doesn't get into the Soul. Everything below the Soul is a stepped-down energy.

Interviewer: That has a lot to do with energy, because there's some kind of energy going on then in that transfer.

J-R: Not necessarily energy in terms of electricity or water, but energy more as life. What makes your heart beat? An energy. We're talking about that energy that makes your heart beat. It's very hard to discuss.

I call those levels below Soul the ten percent. The ninety percent is all that you can't perceive with the physical senses. You can't see it, though you can be aware of it. You can see its manifestation, which is hard to do physically, but spiritually you can see it very clearly.

Interviewer: In some systems of theology, there are rational proofs for God's existence that sometimes seem to be an effort to bridge the gap between faith and reason. Would you say a little bit about that?

J-R: Reasoning has a reference point behind it, usually empirically or experientially based. Faith is based more upon the imagination. The imagination can produce all sorts of strange and peculiar things. Let's say that any power can be gauged between a one and a ten. I'd give reasoning a two, and I'd give faith an eight, because of the power behind it and what it can do. Faith is as real an energy to me as is touching something. Reasoning isn't as real. I can't change the faith energy-field, but I can change the reasoning energy-field.

Interviewer: Do you think of MSIA as new age?

J-R: I think of us as new vocabulary on old information. In a lot of seminars I've done, people have said, "That's really ancient, traditional information. I never knew you studied it."

I haven't studied it. It's in all the traditions, though it may not be the primary focus. One of the things we emphasize is the Sound Current, which is described by Jesus as "the wind." That is one of the ways that the Sound Current is perceived: as wind.

Interviewer: That's one of my favorite passages in John: "The wind blows where it will..."

J-R: And, "those who can hear, let them hear." You can go through the Bible and pick out forty or fifty places where you could substitute the word "sound," or "Sound Current" for this concept of the wind. Why is it said like that? The people at that time used a whole different vocabulary from ours today.

Interviewer: One of the things I find fascinating about those parts of the New Testament is that the word for Spirit and wind is the very same word in the regional language of the time. I think there's way too much separation in a lot of religious thought between the wind in nature and the Spirit of God.

J-R: Well, if you asked me what I thought of that, I'd say I think that the wind, as the Spirit of God, and the wind of nature are really the same thing.

One of the things that traditionally happens when we start doing spiritual work is that people go right out of their body. Many people find it hard to stay here. You'll see their heads nodding, and it looks like they might be asleep. They could be asleep, it's a great masquerade. But often you can say their name and they'll snap right back here. They were present, but to another level.

Interviewer: In the introduction of Jim Lewis' book, Seeking the Light, *he talked about that and I found it fascinating.*

J-R: "Dozing into the Light."

Interviewer: I have looked at parts of the book, and he seems to be open-minded.

J-R: We wouldn't have let him do it if he wasn't open-minded to look at everything. One of our things was: you must look at everything.

Interviewer: He seems to have a open-minded, open-hearted project in mind in trying to get out the ideas in MSIA.

J-R: I thought Jim Lewis did a good job. Many people ask me about religion and I tell them, "Go talk to your priest," because I don't deal in religion. The priest is going to know a lot more in three seconds than I'm going to know all day long. Jim knew more about what we were doing from the academic persuasion than we did being in it. As I read many of the things that he wrote, I thought, "That's the way to say that."

Interviewer: I don't see in the writings that having a specifically defined idea of God is important for you.

J-R: I think that if we can define it, that's not who we're talking about. If we do define it in some way, then we're lying by definition, because He's so much bigger than that.

John Morton: One way we express a definition about God is, "Out of God come all things," and "God loves all of Its creation." I put that together and interpret it to mean that God is everything, and God loves everything.

Our point of view is that when we move into our consciousness of God, our awareness of God, we move into an experience of oneness. God is not a creator that disowns some part of what creation is. So if you, in your own individuality, point to something and say, "That's not God," or "God wouldn't do anything like that," then your God's too small.

Whatever you're looking at is a part of God's creation and God's way of looking at it is through love. This is something that I find differentiates MSIA from a lot of other approaches. When I first encountered that concept, that all things are part of God, and that God loves it all, I had an immediate resonance with it, though I'd never thought in those terms before.

One of the basic teachings is to check things out. Don't go on a belief system. Everyone has a responsibility to have their own experience. That doesn't mean that you follow everything to the nth degree. The way I look at it is that there's a lot that's not my level of concern. It would be like us going outside and trying to direct traffic. Why would we do that? Who assigned us traffic?

Yet we often assign ourselves things that are not our level of concern. That's how we voluntarily lower our nature, getting involved in things that are less than who we are, that make us petty and small when we're much larger than that. Just about one hundred percent of the time, it's unnecessary to follow the things that upset and disturb people. It's understandable that we might react that way through our compassion.

I have children, and if my children are hurt, it's disturbing. I have a place of understanding and acceptance toward that, but I can also be very aware of my own disturbance. I also know that if I were to, let's say, kill the messenger who told me that my child was hurt, that would be an extreme reaction to the upset.

So a lot of what we're dealing with is what I consider a range of consciousness. If we move into a very high state of awareness, a spiritual state, then we become detached from the material world. That spiritual awareness allows us the opportunity to be very accepting, or even completely accepting. As soon as we move our awareness and we're more aware of the flesh, then we're more aware of the hurt physically, emotionally and mentally

I've seen movies in which there's an attempt to portray an unconscious or dream-state. Everything is vague, nondescript, seemingly unreal. As the person comes more into the physical reality, they pick up the intensity of this level. It's like crashing, and boom, and bang, and you get the sense that the material world is a very intense experience.

The spiritual world has a different kind of intensity that is vast and non-material. It has much more space in it. The advantage of having that awareness is that we can look at things from a place of altitude. In a higher state, we can look at the physical and see what is called for and what really is an appropriate action in the circumstances. When we become more aware of ourselves in the physical world, we can direct ourself into the right and proper action, versus a reaction that's based on disturbance, anger, sadness or that type of thing.

What is the Spirit? It's an unseen, intangible consciousness, and yet it's an absolute intelligence, an absolute awareness. It is also invisible. That's one way I relate to the Spirit. Its nature is not bound by things that are physical or psychic. It's as though the Spirit is running through all the psychic-material worlds freely, uninhibited, uncontrolled. The Spirit is not subservient to the psychic-material worlds, but is in it.

That is a key awareness for me, that there is this nature of God that is a very pure, clear aspect, and that is called the Spirit. If I move my consciousness into the Spirit, it would afford me great benefit. For me there's a selfishness in this involvement. Why would I want to spend my time doing this instead of earning a lot of money, or going out and doing things that are pleasurable and all of that. For me, there was great value in knowing how to circumvent a lot of what goes on in the world.

I saw a lot of reactiveness in myself and in others. It is a chaotic condition: people making mistakes, knowing they were making mistakes, doing things that they regretted doing, knowing that in the moment and yet not being able to stop. I was looking for something that would allow me to get free of the reactive state.

At first, when I was reading John-Roger's books and listening to the tapes, it was theory. It sounded good, and it was a good read. But how was I to really know it? Clearly, the only way to discover that was to become involved. What I found was that it checked out. Did it check out perfectly? It checked out enough and there was an allowance for what gets lost in the translation.

J-R or any teacher of the Spirit are sharing what they hear and see, and it's something that we don't necessarily hear or see. They have an understanding or experience of what it is and they're translating it to us. What if something is mis-translated? The process is not quite literal, and something *is* being lost in the translation. I've heard J-R say many times, "As soon as I utter it, I'm lying. I'm mis-saying." So it's not based on having the words be a hundred percent accurate and true.

Why do we go on and do this anyway, sharing in the best way we can? There's a value in the attempt. There is an understanding that mis-translation is part of this process, but that I can, out of my own spiritual nature, bypass that and touch into the truth of what is being said. That's really what is being taught.

J-R: You have to catch the Spirit, or have the Spirit catch you.

John Morton: The God in me will know what's true. Why attempt to become what J-R is, flesh and blood? That's not going to happen, that's not in my destiny. But there is something else there. There's a God-force, or a God consciousness in him that vibrates my God consciousness. There's a reason why John-Roger, in particular, vibrates my God consciousness. I look at that as a spiritual directive. What I've observed is that it's no accident when people are turned away from this Movement. They're really being directed into something else. We're not here to say, "This is *the* way." For my consciousness, it is the way, and I have a responsibility to that experience.

J-R: One reason we don't go into great detail about our experiences is because of the human factor of making comparisons. You'll start to look for who his God is. By measuring your God against his God, you may find yourself coming up short and feel bad, or find yourself much, much larger and look at him as being inferior. Neither one of those are what we want to deal with.

I preface what I say with, "This has been my experience." You can look at the arrow to see if you want to go that way. You must walk your own path and have your own experience. When you get to the experience of God that is for you to have, you will understand and appreciate what the others have, and how they've evolved themselves vibratorily into the Spirit. You'll have a tremendous honoring and respect for even the most minor one who does anything, because it is not easy. It's simple, but it is not simplistic.

It's rapid because it's direct. It's like, take in a deep breath and be God. That's pretty direct. In MSIA, we say, "And on your second breath, feel God again. And the third one, again, and deeper." So it's a worship of something that is worthy to worship. If we don't feel worthy, God is worthy. So we worship what is worthy to be worshipped. It could be a human being. Like sometimes a little baby is so worthy, you look at it, and you just love them and worship them, and you're at their beck and call.

A lot of people's self-esteem is low because they're basing their whole existence only upon themself and the failure of their experiences, rather than upon themself, the failure of the experiences, and the wisdom gained from the failure. The wisdom gained is the self-esteem. That's really a great thing.

Interviewer: Are the Souls eternal or were they created or emanated by God at some point in time?

John Morton: Souls are individualized. That's one way to look at a Soul, that it has a self. Is it outside of God? Is a finger outside of the body? No. You could look at a finger as having it's own life, in a way. It's a finger. So we identify it. The Soul has an individuality.

Interviewer: What you are telling me is, there was a creation, but we don't know very much about it from our human perspective.

John Morton: I look at where we are as a very minute aspect of it, very individualized, very material. It's concrete, it's the way that we relate to ourselves physically. In terms of the relationship to a totality of God, it's virtually nothing. And yet, we relate to ourselves individually as though it's everything.

Interviewer: You say that Souls came here, into the material universe, because they made a conscious decision to come. If it's a conscious decision, that means they might have decided otherwise.

John Morton: It's a free choice. That's the way I look at it. I think that once the Soul incarnates, then there are some have-to's that begin to show up karmically, where the person's karma dictates re-embodiment.

Interviewer: Are the Souls who don't incarnate related to the origin of angels?

John Morton: No, I think you can look at angels as another form, another individualization of God. There's an angelic kingdom or world, a reality of angels who function on that frequency or vibration.

Interviewer: I would like to understand how these two points of your theology go together. One is "Not one Soul will be lost." And the other is, "Even the Soul will be transcended." Is that like nirvana in Eastern philosophy, meaning all Souls will coalesce into the one God in the end?

John Morton: The psychic-material worlds will be pulled up and returned to Spirit. If we're talking to you as a Soul, we'd say that your true home is Soul. That's your true nature, that's your true reality. You come into this world as a visitor; this is not your true home.

Interviewer: But will the Soul maintain some sort of individuality forever, or will it merge into God and lose his or her individuality?

J-R: If you use the word "individuality," then the conversation has to stop. But if you ask if the Soul retains its wisdom, then I suggest that we retain everything we learn. You will have access to that wisdom.

Interviewer: So it's different from the Buddhist idea that you as you are entirely annihilated into God.

J-R: I think we're up against words here, rather than what is. Right here, right now, we are what we have always been. Always. So, if we're going to be in God, we are already in God. If we're going to have individual wisdom, we already have that in God. And if we're going to blend into God, then we're already in God. We're expressing what is spiritual into a material form. That's the difficulty in the spiritual life—getting the spiritual part down and out here, where it's more usable.

Interviewer: Which brings me to my next question. Can you say anything about the Preceptor Consciousness?

J-R: The Preceptor Consciousness should probably never have been brought up or mentioned, because it's so difficult to put into words—it's outside of creation. It's what holds all creation. It's like a balloon holding everything inside the balloon. This is a very strange thing, though the experience is available. It's similar to when you're driving your car down the road thinking about something else and you miss your exit. You may go a few miles further and suddenly wonder where you are and what's going on. You have to wonder where you were when you missed the turnoff that you've taken every day and know so well. You may say, "I don't remember. I was someplace but I don't remember where." You could have just described the Preceptor Consciousness with that.

I tell people that they would be further ahead not to use that name because you're dealing with something that has no real vocabulary to define it. It's outside of creation and you can't even say it's outside of creation. My blundering attempt to give something to people that they could understand has ended with them giving up trying to comprehend it; they just say the words. People refer to the "Mystical Traveler/Preceptor Consciousness." It's nice, it has a rhythm to it, though they could just as well say, "The Traveler."

It's like asking, "What's the Soul?" If you asked me that, I'd say it's an energy unit. That's what I said to a scientist who was interviewing me; he asked me to tell him in scientific terms, and I told him, "It's an energy unit." I can't say, "the All of the All" or "the It of Itself," because those don't do it either. So I came up with the idea that the Soul is who breathes you and who wakes you and sleeps you, who digests all your food and runs your blood and beats your heart when you don't know how. And it's bigger than that. When you're there, it is certainly the most joyful, carefree attitude there is; everything is just really fine.

Interviewer: Would you speak of it as creation?

J-R: I would say this: everything is already created, but not everything is transformed. All creation is not yet manifested, but all creation is created. That may have to come down through molecules, minerals, whatever. It may come down through, let's use the word, superior beings, who may come here to show us the next step that we embrace. Much like going from candles to electricity. It would be a real evolution, the Light will really come on bright. When God said, "It's done, it's good," I took Him at His word.

John Morton: You remind me of that film, "The Day the Earth Stood Still," with Michael Renney and Gort. Gort was the inter-galactic enforcer. This being basically landed in a spaceship in Washington, D.C., or somewhere like that, and of course, the initial reaction was that they were under attack. Gradually, people realized that what he was making clear to the human form was that there was another way. The message was basically that the planet had to get along better and stop the process of war. Since the technology had developed so people could blow one another to smithereens, the importance of changing consciousness was on the planet.

I often think that's a lot of what's going on in the Movement of Spiritual Inner Awareness; in a twinkling of the eye, a person realizes themselves. They're not in this world to survive, to have great achievements, and the typical things that we look out and see people doing. That really is not what's serving fulfillment. Fulfillment is an awakening process and the Traveler Consciousness is a consciousness that takes those who awaken to the Spirit and moves them. It brings experiences that create greater understanding of the Divine Heritage that is the destiny as a Soul. A person involved in this starts relating to life as a Soul instead of an animalistic creature that's trying to get the best furniture, the best apartment, etc. The motivation shifts.

Historically, those are often people who end up serving humanity in some way. People who have been awakened to their Spirit end up serving somehow. They may be a great writer, they may be someone who causes change. The change may not always be pleasant, but it's necessary.

Interviewer: In reading through the material, I was struck by how important it is to do the spiritual exercises and service.

J-R: It's important to do spiritual exercises if you want to see in the Spirit what is going on with your spiritual travels. The highest consciousness on the planet that you can see demonstrated is that of service. So we believe in service and doing spiritual exercises. But prior to that, it should be said, "If you want to know." If you don't, you can still do all of the spiritual work without opening your spiritual eyes. The Traveler Consciousness is on that side working with you in your Soul and your Spirit.

Interviewer: How do you see the importance of service in one's spiritual life?

J-R: Oh, just really tantamount to number one. There are two spiritual lives. There is yours inwardly and what you do, and then there is yours out here in the world and what you do. Inwardly, there is what you do traveling in the Sound Current and the Light, following the Lord; those are all one. Service comes from when Jesus said, "When you've done it to the least one of these, you've done it unto me." That puts service out there in the world as number one. That's where those two come from. There are others: "Love your neighbor as yourself," and "Love God with your body, mind and Soul." Right there is the inner and the outer.

Interviewer: Are there other things that you really consider essential behavior?

John Morton: There is a primary directive and it is loving. If you want an application that would bring you into an awareness, into an alignment with the Movement of Spiritual Inner Awareness, with Soul Transcendence, I would say to you, be loving. Do it more than you've ever done before. That is actually what's available to you this moment, for you to experience yourself in greater loving than you've ever experienced.

When things come to you that challenge you, stay in loving rather than react in a closed-off or negative way. Part of that is a neutral state. Sometimes it's just being open; then whatever is going on will take you as a state of neutrality. It isn't about doing. It's about letting go of the inner mental and emotional attachments. The place where we have the greater opportunities and challenges is in the inner consciousness. The real spiritual victory takes place inside.

What we do out here has influence. If we do something negative, we have responsibility for what we've done. But spiritually it's not like, "Because of that, I'm sorry, you're out." We know how to let the situation go, and then we let go of the judgment, which is often what people don't know how to release. When we work with people, that's a lot of what we're focusing upon. How are you judging? How are you hanging on? How are you attached so that you're not free? The consciousness of Spirit is a free consciousness. It's not attached to anything. It's not bound by anything. If you're holding on and can't get by something, that's what we work with.

Interviewer: I'd like to hear how you view God in relation to love. Could one say that God is love?

J-R: Love is an essence that keeps us in relative relationship to each other. We don't know if that's close or far away, because it's relative. To a husband

and wife, it's closer; to, let's say, us and somebody in Russia, it's further away. It still could be love, it's just a relative distance. I think it's the Spirit of God. Not God as God, but God's Spirit that moves out through everything and keeps us going. That love is the key to it as far as we know here, physically.

John Morton: For me, probably one of the greatest scriptures from the Bible is from 1st John: "God is love, and he who dwells in love dwells in God, and God in him," and when Jesus said, "How will they know you're my disciples? That ye love one another. I give you a new commandment, that ye do love one another as I have loved you."

It's always been spoken in very bold terms that the way to recognize the Movement of Spiritual Inner Awareness is in the loving. Love is about as good a word as you can put on the essence of what this is. How do you recognize it and how do you know it's in action? People are flowing with their Spirit, and it's in the loving.

People put all kinds of forms on love. You can be in conflict with someone and say, "I'm doing this because I love you and because you really need this." You're not loving the person, but you're calling it love.

J-R: You're beating up on them.

John Morton: I've heard J-R talk about another great commandment many times: "Do unto others as you would have them do unto you." You look at someone and think, "I don't want them doing unto me the way they do unto themselves." People don't necessarily love themselves or one another. It takes a great demonstration for someone to really be a clear example of love.

J-R: That quote John mentioned is interpretive. I say it this way: "Do unto me as I would have done unto me. If you want to know what that is, I'll tell you." I wouldn't want some people to love me like they're loving, because they just might kill me. They'll beat you up, and it's all "for your own good."

Our job with children is to help them go through their destiny, not to transform their destiny to our way of thinking and doing, and if they don't, then they get punishment. I don't think that's asking the child to honor and obey you. I think it's asking a child to leave as soon as possible.

When John's daughter Claire says she wants to do something, it's not my job to say, "No, you can't. I've looked at it carefully already through experience." It's, "How do you want to do that?" and let her go about using me as a sounding board. I question what she says she wants to do to see if we are going to be able to do it together. Sometimes I'll say,

"No, you've got to talk to your dad or your mom about that." That's the person to talk to, because they're the ones who have authority in that area. In other areas, they don't. The one who has authority is the one who's there willing to support the action and to keep it going toward where the child's destiny is.

Since you don't know exactly what their destiny is, you must pay close attention to what your children are doing. This is called monitoring, babysitting, and being involved with your child. There are all sorts of techniques for doing that.

One technique that I use with Claire is to say, "How was school today?"

She'll say, "Oh, it was all right."

I'll say, "So you want to do exactly the same thing tomorrow?"

She'll say, "Well, no."

I'll ask, "What was it that you didn't like today that you don't want to do tomorrow?"

She'll tell me. And I get to know what happened today.

Then I'll ask, "Was there anything you want to do tomorrow that carried over from today?"

She'll say, "Oh, yeah!" Then I get to find out what she's doing and how her friends are approaching it. I don't need a long time with this because we've done it so often that she knows the game of participation.

I've looked at her and said, "What kind of music is so-and-so?" and she'll tell me. A couple times, she's said, "I don't think of them as music."

I'll ask her, "What do you think of them as?" and she'll come up with something that's really good.

The brilliance that a youngster will bring forward when allowed to is, to me, worthy of worship. It isn't a ritualistic approach as much as it is one of welcoming them forward to participate and tell you, and to honor what they're saying. If they say things that don't make sense, draw that to their attention. Tell them that you're not getting the sense out of what they're saying and see if they can rephrase it. There's a constant dialogue going on. To me, that's part of the Movement of Spiritual Inner Awareness as a real practical, here and now application.

The children around us, and I'm sure this is so in other places, will come up and say things that we didn't find out until we were thirty years old. They're coming up with it at eight, and you'll be wondering, "Who told them that?" Once Claire told me something and I said, "How did you know that?"

She said, "My mind told me."

I said, "Okay."

She asked me, "Why? Do you have a question about that?"

I said, "No, Claire, because I think your mind is probably real good. If you were ten or fifteen years older, I might want us both to question what your mind was saying to see that it's producing for you what you really want and what you want others to want or have around you."

She said, "Okay." There were no have to's.

She's ahead of me. This happened when she was about four years old

Interviewer: It's helpful to hear how the teachings have a practical application.

J-R: If it's not practical, if you can't work it, why bother with it. If it works for you, use it; if it doesn't, have the wit to let it go. It might work on Monday, and not Tuesday, and then pick up again on Thursday. You have to keep your wits about you, which doesn't allow you to go into a stupor or a presumed intelligence about how something works.

Some people say, "God is the same yesterday, today, and tomorrow." Nobody knows that to be true, though it's a very clever statement. They've defined God that way. I don't think God fits a definition at all. If you said, "What's your definition of God?" I'd have to say, "God is God." I have no more definition than that. I can tell you more about the experiences of God. God loves all Its creation, out of God come all things, and not one Soul will be lost. I can tell you how that works down here. Take care of yourself, so you can help take care of others. Don't hurt yourself, and don't hurt others. And use everything for your advancement, upliftment and growing.

And then what? Then we work for health, wealth, and happiness, prosperity, abundance and riches, loving, caring, and sharing, and touching to people with all that.

So there's something like a theology in this. Those are the guidelines, not the rules. Maybe someone's in a situation and not seeing what they could learn from it. It may be that they're so stressed emotionally or ego-wise that there's no way they can perceive the learning at the moment. Let them have the experience until they get through it, process it and come out of it. Then they may find that they can learn from the experience.

There aren't any timelines on people's behavior. If we look at karma as being something that has relevance—cause and effect—who is to know how long someone's karma runs, or what they're to get out of it, or what the message is?

People have asked me, "How do I know what my karma is?"

I say, "What do you do all or most of the time?" They'll tell me and I'll say, "That's your karma." If they say, "But I do other things," well, there's more than one karma.

As soon as we learn what that is, we automatically change it because we get bored. Boredom is the thing that says, "Now move." I look at boredom as a valuable signpost indicating that it's time to get to the next thing, or time's up.

If something is boring to me and others are still into it, I'll stay with them because of companionship. I don't necessarily look at that as loving, just companionship. We may be together in the same room, or we may just see each other periodically two or three times a week at work. As far as they're concerned, I'm doing the same thing. But as soon as I see them getting discontented, I ask, "Are you experiencing this, this, this, this?"

If they say, "Yes, I'm tired and I want to go," I'll say, "Great. I'm ready." They'll often ask me how long I've been ready, and I'll say, "A while back." If you say, "Three years ago, I'm just waiting for you," that is a put-down. Since we work with, "Don't hurt yourself and don't hurt others," you say the same truth without referencing it back negatively to the other person.

Interviewer: Would you talk more about the influence of Spirit in your life?

John Morton: My sense of Spirit and how it influences us pretty much most of the time is that it's a really quiet, still voice. The quality that I most associate with

Spirit is something very quiet, silent, unobtrusive, subtle. It takes a great sensitivity to be aware of it's movement. To listen to where the noise is, or to where the hustle and the bustle are is to distract yourself. Spirit may work through those things, like it works in everything. Some people look at having a powerful feeling, or a great passion as a sign of the presence of Spirit. I don't associate with it that way. I would tend to tell someone not to look there, but rather to pray quietly.

That's also a place in scripture that says not to attempt to become pious by having the best seats in the congregation or recognition in some way. That's not just a personal thing to me, it is something about MSIA as a practice where I would say we teach people to be humble in the way they approach Spirit. We basically encourage people not to disclose their personal experiences from their prayers and spiritual exercises. That will mislead others and tempt them to worship recognition and false things rather than something that is very personal. There are occasions where we are called upon to disclose and reveal the sacredness of the experience, the holiness, and the joy, and the passion. Those are more rare than what is ongoing.

Interviewer: What is the difference between the Christ and the Mystical Traveler?

John Morton: Both the Traveler and the Christ represent a turning point. Jesus was holding the office of the Christ, which is a door, a gate, a turning point from the negative into the positive. In this world, the Christ is doing what the Traveler is doing. There's complete cooperation, collaboration, if you will. There's no issue, there's no conflict, it's just a job to be done and it's being done spiritually. We all have an ability or let's say an opportunity to become Christ. In the moment, we could be seen as the Christ and we could be transmitting the Christ. Someone might say, so-and-so is the Christ, I know he's the Christ, I saw him doing these things and I saw Jesus on his face; this is the Christ come. That person may turn around and do all the things you would do when you're not the Christ, and you'll be wondering, "What's going on?" We have our moments when we're in our glory, and we have our moments when we stink. The difference with Jesus is the degree of excellence. I don't find a higher mark.

We look at Jesus as a Traveler. The Christ is looked upon as a savior of people who, because of their transgressions, were bound karmically to the planet. John-Roger was saying that it has to do with the planet. The three days from the point of the crucifixion was a time of release of what was earthbound. Those who were earthbound from previous times had an opportunity to hear and see the one who was releasing them. Any consciousness that would turn toward the Light would not be denied; the negativity could no longer bind them. I see that represented on the day of the crucifixion with the murderer who turned and said, "Can you do something for me?" The response was, "I'll see you in Paradise today." To me, the murderer represented the worst, the darkest, turning to the Light; if they would turn, they were allowed instant access. It is a consciousness of grace that allows for that.

It's also the having the wit to ask. There was another one on the cross who didn't ask. What was being represented to us was that some choose into it and some don't. The Traveler represents a consciousness of the Soul that is allowing those who seek their spiritual heritage to return into their Soul nature, to realize their Soul nature, and to establish themselves in the Soul realm of consciousness so that the true home is not of this world. The true home is of the Soul. That's where we come from, that's where we're going, and the Traveler is the consciousness of a wayshower that allows people access into that.

When people step into the Christ, it's a consciousness of following. It's a consciousness of, "This too you shall do." A person must take hold of their anointed nature. Christ is one who demonstrated that, and holds that consciousness. He was one who came in the flesh and transmitted the reality that we can choose positively, we can choose spiritually, we can choose the Light. With that comes great responsibility.

Interviewer: If I hear what you're saying correctly, something ontologically happened when Christ, when Jesus went through the crucifixion experience. There was actually a change in the cosmos.

John Morton: Yes. I see that it was a time of redemption, but not just in terms of Jesus. Jesus had to come in through the flesh and take on the temptations that we all are subjected to, so that it couldn't be said, "He was elect, so it's not fair. He was God's son, so God was always protecting him and not allowing the difficulties and the things that us poor mortals have to deal with." It was set up so that you couldn't miss that he was dealing with what we are dealing with. It's just that he had a state of consciousness, a state of awareness that was obviously immeasurable.

Interviewer: And the effect for us is that we now have a choice to turn to the Light, when we were previously bound in darkness.

John Morton: Yes. There were Masters who were walking in the Light prior to Jesus. The difference is that he did something that was for the planet, that was established on the planet at that point. Prior to that, people were limited to the law of cause and effect.

Because people kept accruing negativity through their actions, from a Soul standpoint, they kept building up a karmic debt and in a sense were earth-bound forever. They were in eternal hell. Once we get caught in a negative cycle, it is very difficult to change. Something had to be done. It was a shift in what was allowed; people were allowed to see the Light directly despite their negativity. If the person, in their ignorance, still chose darkness, Jesus said, "I can help all but the fools. You've got to choose into this, you've got to choose back. I can show it to you, I can demonstrate it to you, I can let you see it and feel it." He removed blindness and deafness, whatever all the miracles were. But according to the accounts, there were still those who were saying, "I just don't believe it." There was Thomas, "I'm not sure, I'm not sure." I look at that as the nature of the mind. When we're in the field of illusion, we don't see what is. We have doubt. We have fear that influences our ability to respond.

Interviewer: Who is Jesus in relation to the Christ and the Mystical Traveler Consciousness? Are those related?

J-R: Sure. You could look at Jesus as a model and Christ as the way and the Traveler as a conveyor belt, as a mechanism.

Interviewer: And they work together?

J-R: Three in one. We look at Jesus Christ as the CEO of the organization. He's my boss. I have contact, communication, direction with Jesus Christ as often or as constantly as I wish. In an instant, in a second, for demonstration, for show, for pleasure, for whatever. But not for abuse or misuse, or to try to confuse someone or confound them, because of the nature of who Jesus Christ is in the Spirit, and how it represents down through me and the office that I held as the Traveler. The Traveler's almost like dirt, it's all over, and Jesus Christ walked through the body of Jesus on the road. One is a foundational aspect, but it's in direct contact with the Christ Consciousness as personified through Jesus.

I think that when you die and you go to heaven, St. Peter, or whoever is reputed to be the keeper of the Book of Life, will not want to know if you led the life of Jesus Christ. I think he's going to ask if you did you, the Christ. Jesus already did Jesus the

Christ. You are to do yours. When you do that, you are an inheritor of the Kingdom. If you don't do yours, you would not be an inheritor of the Kingdom. How do we know that scripturally? If we take Jesus at his word, he said, "This that I do, you, too, shall do and even greater, because I go to the Father."

It might be even more so because he really was like a Johnny Appleseed. He planted and never really got to eat of his own plantings. That was left for all of us later on. All through the ages since he lived, we've been receiving the seeds of his planting.

I think he allowed the engrafting of many things into it so that we get all sorts of variations, as I think were in the Garden of Eden. I don't think it was a garden of weeding, I think that it was a purposeful setup to have the archetype of everything that is to be and will be. I'm not too sure it was in the physical world, though I think it probably had a physical anchor; but it went up kind of high.

Interviewer: I read about the Traveler Consciousness as an anchor, a wayshower which is one of the ways that Spirit relates to the physical world.

J-R: One of the ways. The Traveler Consciousness performs a very specific function: Soul Transcendence. Its nature is eternal wisdom, something that always has been, the foundation of all things that are. When God spoke, He spoke upon the concept of the Traveler. Not as we know it here, not just this universe, but through anything that exists. I know of over a hundred and eight universes, and that's just on this issuance. Some of them have been pulled back up already and others issued forth. I don't know if you'd call that evolution, or God mucking around and making a lot of mistakes. Or maybe these are the opportunities that keep appearing for man to grow and learn, and for God to keep expressing God as God.

Many people open to Spirit for a second and gestalt it. It may then take years for them to unwind that gestalting so that it makes practical sense to them to continue on with it. Some people see the Light and are blinded by it. They turn away because it was too bright. It's like somebody shining a very bright light right into your eyes; you turn away. It's involuntary until you learn that the Light can come at any time or place, with anyone, with anything. That makes you tolerant of all races, religions, creeds, and colors because the Light can come out of any one of them. So you have to keep your eyes open.

We have a tape called, "Observation, the Key to Letting Go," which describes a key element in the Movement: keep watching. We don't do belief, we do experience. Belief is comprehension, a mental concept; understanding is the wisdom you've gained from your physical actions and life, often through the mistakes you've made.

John Morton: The anchoring sounds like a very heavy word, or a word that doesn't have much function in it. If you look at what the anchoring is doing, you're not going to find much there. It's not for the purpose of seeing an anchor, it's for the purpose of taking what is from another dimension into this dimension and holding it here in a form that's functioning. The anchor is allowing the conveyor belt, as we referred to it, to be turned on for those who will avail themselves of it.

If Christ is the way, then why is there this conveyor belt? It's an added function that's now moving at a higher rate. It's still working through the Christ, through an access of Spirit by which every Soul is quickened. Something happens in that presence that is a conviction. That's one way I look at it: that we're convicted by the Spirit. What happens? Our illusions are convicted by the Spirit as false. If we don't have the wit to let go of our false identification, then we go with it.

It's as though the Christ comes in and starts cleaning house. What's false leaves, and if a person doesn't have the wit to let go of their false identification, then they go out with that falsehood, and they go where that goes. If they do have the wit, then they come into a truth of their conviction which can be very powerful; it's like being born in the Spirit, humbled, made new. It's a very deep experience of being resurrected in our truth. We rise up in our truth and what is false must go.

The Traveler Consciousness makes that an ongoing process. What if a person was born again and had been convicted in the Spirit, and now they're stealing, robbing, cheating, pillaging and raping? What happened to that spiritually convicted person? There's an ongoing conviction that we identify as a loyalty, a dedication to the Soul. A person who recognizes their spirituality and realizes that they want to make a commitment toward that is making a commitment toward truthful living. According to the world? No. According to how Spirit reveals it to them inside. The loyalty is not to John-Roger or to MSIA as an organization.

J-R: It's certainly not taught, but it may be there.

John Morton: Is there thankfulness? Gratitude? A recognition that the Traveler is a fountain, a source? Yes. I looked at John-Roger as my teacher and my wayshower because that's how it was revealed to me inside. Do I then have some kind of assignment to do that for you? No. As a person who's anchoring this consciousness, this conveyor belt, I look at the Spirit as the one who will convict us of what is true in our consciousness.

If that conviction brings you here, knocking on the door saying, "What do you have for me? What do you know?," I would be practical and ask if you have listened to the tapes and read the Discourses. That is a way that you can bring in the information and start working it. So as an anchor, I'm free from the responsibility to have a personal relationship with everyone. At the same time, the way it works on a practical level is that we do continually make ourselves available, in the newness of what it is.

There is a continual presentation, but we often tell people, "This is in the first Discourse. This is in every seminar. The likelihood that you're going to hear something new tonight is slim. What you may hear is a new interpretation." You might say, "That's the interpretation I've been looking for and waiting for all these years." The reality is that the essence has been spoken all along. It's just being repeated in not so new ways. What is it that we're really saying? People tell us that we're not saying anything new, that we're just borrowing from here and there. My response is that the truth has no address unless it's everywhere.

The reality is that there is a dynamic in MSIA that I haven't experienced elsewhere. The responsibility is clearly placed on each person to check things out and validate them for themself. We often say that MSIA is a group of non-joiners, people who backed into one another because they were backing away from all these other forms that are out there. We find ourselves in a quadrant of people who are independent and have done a lot of self-processing, looking and considering. MSIA is not usually their initial effort in adapting something religiously or spiritually. I like that. And we have our range of individuals and personalities that you're going to find in any group.

J-R: I think if you really took a slice out of humanity, you would find the Movement of Spiritual Inner Awareness in there. If you were to take a slice through this Movement of Spiritual Inner Awareness, you'd find all of humanity.

John Morton: There's a seminar that John-Roger did early on called, "Ordinariness—A Prior Condition to God." It covers a lot about how I view the Movement of Spiritual Inner Awareness. In this Movement, rather than becoming exalted or somehow special, we take off the veneer and pretense and we find that we're all human in our basic nature. When there's a willingness to do this with honesty as part of our practice, joy comes present. There is a lot of laughter and joy around what we do and the people who are involved in what we're doing. We have a good time even though there's a fair amount of criticism, judgment, cynicism and sarcasm directed at us.

One of the measures I've found in this Movement is that, if you're doing this because of pride or for recognition, you can't last very long. There's a lot of opportunity in our gatherings for people to share about things that are bothering them that maybe they're embarrassed about. After you've heard from enough people, you realize that everyone has something, there are no perfect individuals walking around here. There's a wonderful closeness that happens because all those things just don't matter. We are not people who aim to judge. We certainly encourage people to learn, to grow, to make better choices. We process a lot of individual situations in very open ways. It'd be like you telling what is most bothersome or embarrassing to you in front of hundreds of people. You might think that you would never choose to do that, but there's so much value in your willingness to share and be vulnerable. Something quite magical often happens to people who do this, so that they're transformed.

J-R: I've seen more people walk away free than ever walked away more confined. We'll bring people back up and say, "We're not through yet. You're still too tight." If they'll finally tell what is bothering them, they'll often also say, "I never would have said that in my whole life, and now I've just told everybody."

John Morton: I sometimes wonder if the people who invented talk shows ran into one of our groups and said, "Great idea. We'll get people in front of national audiences and have them tell their stories. It'll be entertaining and we'll get lots of people watching because something happens." A lot of talk shows are helpful because they're getting issues that have been suppressed out in the open; at least they're being looked at even if they're also being laughed at. There's something uplifting about people being willing to reveal things that have been hidden.

Our intention is to reflect to people that they are not those behaviors. They're not those conditions and habits and addictions. We let them see that there are other ways that they can handle themselves.

J-R: Ordinariness is such a tremendous key. A lot of people come into our field of action and say, "I didn't get treated like anyone special." If you're after special treatment, you shouldn't be in MSIA, because you're going to get treated just like everyone else. People who have been involved a long time sometimes get upset if they don't get their special whatever. We'll ask, "Why are you upset? Did you become special?" Often they'll own up and say, "Oh, yeah, I did," and everybody laughs. We may give them that seat they wanted anyway because they were honest.

The group isn't limited to just who's in the room because everything is taped. The group could be millions of people at some point. Once someone finds their ordinariness, they stop doing ego-trips and specialness and the Spirit of God is right at hand. I've seen a lot of people lit up with that presence. There's a real joy in watching someone find their own joy. Once one person starts to find it, it's contagious.

"Living in Grace," an annual retreat, was just hilarious. Two to three hundred of us were together for seven days, and we had howls of laughter. One prayer came out something like, "God, please help these people," and everyone just cracked up laughing and couldn't stop. That's right and appropriate for them to do, and the person who was praying just kept right on going, because that was their mission.

Some people lose that ordinariness, thinking they're higher than others because they've been studying a long time. As a matter of fact, the person just coming in could be at a higher vibration, waiting for this whole group to get up to the level where they could find us.

Interviewer: I have noticed that you don't have to hold certain beliefs to become a member of MSIA. There isn't a creed of some sort that you have to follow.

J-R: The Church of the Movement of Spiritual Inner Awareness is not a social organization for social reform in the world. It's moving the spiritual inner awareness. Our business is Soul Transcendence.

Why do we go internally? Because Jesus Christ himself said, "The Kingdom of Heaven is at hand. The Kingdom of Heaven is within. The Father and I are one. And the Father resides in the Kingdom of Heaven." If you can't go in and find that for yourself, all the scriptural references have very little validity for you.

We work for the highest good of all concerned. We don't go for againstness. We are for health, wealth, happiness, prosperity, abundance and riches, loving, caring and sharing. That includes all people even though they're not here. Soul Transcendence is our main thing.

Interviewer: As I've read the Discourses, it seems to me that what's being done here is to invite people to explore their own spiritual side and to come into a relationship with you that occurs at an invisible level.

J-R: Yes.

Interviewer: I'm assuming that what is written and what is said has that as the goal, not the mastering of the material.

J-R: Right. Those are points of attunement.

John Morton: The contact takes place spiritually first and can be there for a long time. People realize that something is going on inside that the world hasn't quite caught up to and they are looking, searching for some way to match it up in the world. It's unrequited until they have that "Eureka, I've found it!" experience. People come in and realize, "This is it, I am home." When they hear a seminar or read a Discourse, there's a familiar sense about it. The reality is that it still has to check out. If I go to believe or adopt something that I don't know, then I've been irresponsible.

We will show you what we know about how you find out for yourself. Here are the spiritual exercises, here are tones. Here is what we know about the Light and here's how you can experience that for yourself.

BIBLIOGRAPHY
BOOKS & TAPES
BY JOHN-ROGER & JOHN MORTON
and Other Information

Items are audio tapes unless otherwise noted. V or VC preceding a number denotes the tape is also available in video format. CD indicates compact disk format. Unless noted as a public tape, tapes are for personal use only. Public tape means that this tape can be shared with others. SAT stands for Soul Awareness Tapes, which are audio tapes of J-R seminars, meditations, and sharings that are sent each month only to SAT subscribers. Once you subscribe to SAT, you can obtain previously issued SAT tapes.

AUDIO & VIDEOTAPES
ANI-HU (MUSIC AND MEDITATION)
by John-Roger (#1610, public tape)

ARE YOU DOING GOD'S WILL?
by John-Roger (#7674, SAT tape)

ARE YOU LIVING UNDER LAW OR GRACE?
by John-Roger (#7341, #V -7341, public tape)

ARE YOU THE SPIRITUAL SKY?
by John-Roger (#3008, public tape)

ARE YOU WILLING TO BE GOD
by John Morton (#7364, public tape)

THE ATTITUDE OF GRATITUDE
by John-Roger (#7551, #VC-7551)

BALANCING GIVING AND TAKING
by John-Roger (#7274, SAT tape)

BASIC INSTRUCTIONS FOR SPIRITUAL EXERCISES
by John-Roger (#7535, SAT tape)

THE BLESSING OF GIVING
by John-Roger (#7014, SAT tape)

BLESSINGS, PRAYERS & INVOCATIONS
by John Morton (#7603, public tape)

CHANTING THE SACRED TONES
by John-Roger (#7001, Spanish/English, public tape)

CHRIST IS FORGIVENESS
by John-Roger (#7287, #V -7287)

CULTS: BRAINWASH, WHITEWASH OR HOGWASH?
by John-Roger (#2150)

DISCOURSES AND THE VALUE OF INTROSPECTION
by John-Roger (#7234)

EVERYDAY SOUL
by John Morton with Laren Bright
(#7707, VC-7707, public tape)

FORGIVENESS THROUGH THE CHRIST (CHRISTMAS '83)
by John-Roger, (#7185, #V -7185)

GOD IS INTENTION
by John-Roger (#7354, #VC-7354)

GOSPEL OF ST. JOHN: SPIRITUAL HERITAGE OF MAN/
THE SPIRITUAL PROMISE
by John-Roger, (#7217)

THE HIERARCHY OF CONSCIOUSNESS
by John-Roger (#7114, SAT tape)

HONORING THE BELOVED
by John-Roger (#7311, #V-7311)

HOW CAN WE FOLLOW CHRIST?
by John Morton (#7724, English/Spanish, public tape)

THE HU MEDITATION
by John-Roger (#1800)

IN THE LINE OF TRAVELERS, by John Morton
(#7696, #VC-7696, English/Portuguese, public tape)

INITIATION—MOLDING THE GOLDEN CHALICE
by John-Roger (#2601)

INNER JOURNEY THROUGH SPIRIT REALMS
by John-Roger (#7251)

INNERPHASING FOR MULTIDIMENSIONAL
CONSCIOUSNESS
by John-Roger (#7694)

INTRODUCTION TO MSIA
by John-Roger (#7023)

KEEP GOD AS YOUR FOCUS
by John-Roger (#7425, SAT tape)

LETTING YOU IN
by John Morton (#7339, public tape)

THE LIGHT, THE TRUTH, AND THE WAY
by John-Roger (#7571, one of seven tapes
in the "Spiritual Heritage" series, public tape)

LIVING A NECESSARY LIFE
by John Morton with Laren Bright
(#7700, VC-7700, public tape)

LUXOR MEDITATION FOR PEACE AND HARMONY
by John-Roger (#7303, one of seven PAT IV tapes)

THE MAJESTY OF THE INNER MASTER
by John-Roger (#2625)

MANIFESTING GOD'S ABUNDANCE
by John-Roger (#1477)

THE MASTER AND THE MUDHOLE
by John-Roger (#2612)

MY KINGDOM FOR A HORSE
by John-Roger (#4018)

THE MEDITATION OF THE CHRIST
by John-Roger (#1329)

THE MYSTICAL TRAVELER CONSCIOUSNESS
by John-Roger (#1021)

MYSTICAL TRAVELER: DIRECT LINE TO GOD
by John-Roger (#7127)

NUCLEAR RADIATION FROM GROUND ZERO
by John-Roger (#7061, #VC-7061)

OBSERVATION—THE KEY TO LETTING GO
by John-Roger (#1552, public tape)

PAT V SEMINARS AND MEDITATIONS
by John Morton (#7605, #V-7605, public tape)

PASSAGES TO THE REALMS OF SPIRIT
by John-Roger (#7037)

PERFECT DISCIPLINE IS PERFECT FREEDOM
by John-Roger (#2093)

PLAYING A ROUND WITH GOD
by John Morton (#7537, #V -7537, public tape)

THE POWER OF LOVE
by John-Roger (#2075)

PRACTICAL KEYS TO DOING S.E.'S
by John-Roger (#7193, SAT tape)

PROFOUNDNESS OF THE LOVING HEART
by John-Roger (#7547, #VC-7547)

PROSPERITY BY WAY OF GRACE OR KARMA
by John-Roger (#3412)

PSYCHIC VIOLENCE
by John-Roger (#7308, #V -7308)

REFOCUSING ON GRACE AND LOVING GOD
by John-Roger (#7600, SAT tape)

SEASON OF HARVEST
by John Morton (#7365, public tape)

MSIA INITIATES MEETING TAPES FOR INITIATES ONLY
by John-Roger (Series of 14 tapes, which can be
purchased individually or as a complete set)

MSIA MINISTERS MEETING TAPES FOR MINISTERS ONLY
by John-Roger (Series of 12 tapes, which can be
purchased individually or as a complete set)

SOUND CURRENT
by John-Roger (#2021)

SOUNDS OF THE REALMS
by John-Roger (#2530)

SOUL REALM MOCK-UP AND BEYOND
by John-Roger (#7459, SAT tape)

SPIRIT OF THE EARTH/THE GATHERING
OF PEACEMAKERS
by John Morton and Leigh Taylor-Young
(#5011, public tape)

THE SPIRITUAL WARRIOR/EL GUERRERO ESPIRITUAL
by John-Roger (#7333, #V -7333, English/Spanish)

THOUGHTS, CONSCIOUSNESS, & MANIFESTATION
by John-Roger (#7072)

THE TRAVELER—THE ONE WHO LAUGHS
IN YOUR HEART
by John-Roger (#2602)

TWELVE APPROACHES TO SPIRITUALITY
by John-Roger (#2619, SAT tape)

TWELVE SIGNS OF THE TRAVELER
by John-Roger (#1362, SAT tape)

25 YEARS AS THE TRAVELER
by John-Roger (#V-7311)

UPGRADING OUR ADDICTIONS TO GOD
by John-Roger (#7487, SAT tape)

WHAT DO WE DO FOR LOVE
by John-Roger (#7667, SAT tape)

WHAT IS THE BLESSING OF SOUL TRANSCENDENCE?
by John-Roger (#1131, SAT tape)

WHAT IS SPIRITUAL FASCISM AND TOTALITARIANISM?
by John-Roger (#7036)

WHEN THE MYSTICAL TRAVELER WORKS WITH YOU
by John-Roger (#2053)

TAPE ALBUMS
THE ANOINTED ONE
by John-Roger (Five tape album, #3906)

INNER WORLDS OF MEDITATION
by John-Roger and John Morton
(Six tape album, #3915, #3915-CD, public tape)

LIVING IN GRACE
by John-Roger
(Six tape album, #3903, public tape)

PAT V
by John-Roger and John Morton
(Three tape album, #3912, public tape)

SOUL JOURNEY THROUGH SPIRITUAL EXERCISES
by John-Roger
(Three tape album w/booklet, #3718)

SPIRITUAL EXERCISES INNERPHASING
by John-Roger (Two tape album w/booklet, #3810)

SPIRITUAL EXERCISES: WALKING WITH THE LORD
by John-Roger
(Four tape album with booklet, #3907, public tape)

SPIRITUAL WARRIOR
by John-Roger
(Three tape album, #3908, public tape)

TURNING POINTS TO PERSONAL LIBERATION
by John-Roger
(Six tape album, #3916, public tape)

THE WAYSHOWER
by John Roger
(Two tape album w/booklet, #3901, public tape)

BOOKS
THE BLESSINGS ALREADY ARE
by John Morton (#9JM-1)

THE CHRIST WITHIN & THE DISCIPLES OF CHRIST
WITH THE COSMIC CHRIST CALENDAR
by John-Roger (#935-1)

FORGIVENESS, THE KEY TO THE KINGDOM
by John-Roger (#934-3)

GOD IS YOUR PARTNER
by John-Roger (#927-7)

INNER WORLDS OF MEDITATION
by John-Roger (#977-7)

THE PATH TO MASTERSHIP
by John-Roger (#957-2)

THE POWER WITHIN YOU
by John-Roger (#924-6)

PSYCHIC PROTECTION
by John-Roger (#969-6)

SEEKING THE LIGHT: UNCOVERING THE TRUTH
ABOUT THE MOVEMENT OF SPIRITUAL INNER
AWARENESS AND ITS FOUNDER JOHN-ROGER
by James R. Lewis (#942-4)

SPIRITUAL FAMILY
by John-Roger (#978-5)

SPIRITUAL WARRIOR: THE ART OF SPIRITUAL LIVING
by John-Roger (#936-X, and available at bookstores)

THE TAO OF SPIRIT
by John-Roger (#933-5)

WALKING WITH THE LORD
by John-Roger (#930-0)

MSIA SEMINARS & OTHER EVENTS
John-Roger and John Morton events are advertised in
The New Day Herald.

SOUL TRANSCENDENCE BOOKLET
SOUL TRANSCENDENCE: AN INTRODUCTION TO THE
MOVEMENT OF SPIRITUAL INNER AWARENESS (MSIA)
Describes Discourses and their role in studying with
MSIA, questions and answers about Spirit, lists tapes
recommended for people new to MSIA, and how to
contact MSIA. Can be shared with people not on
Discourses.

PEACE THEOLOGICAL SEMINARY & COLLEGE OF PHILOSOPHY
Classes, Seminars, Retreats, and Trainings

CORRESPONDENCE COURSES
Include Manifesting the Christed Consciousness, Ministry of Service, The Traveler in Your Dreams, Travelers through the Ages, Spiritual Exercises Class, and What is the MSIA Ministry?

MASTER OF SPIRITUAL SCIENCE
A two year program leading to a Master of Spiritual Science degree. First year is entitled Creating Through Grace, year two is entitled Fulfilling the Spiritual Promise.

DOCTOR OF SPIRITUAL SCIENCE
A three year program leading to a Doctor of Spiritual Science degree. A program designed to assist with moving to new levels of expansiveness and awareness.

OTHER SEMINARS, RETREATS AND TRAININGS
Watch for coming events advertised in *The New Day Herald*.

SUBSCRIPTIONS
CHARTER CLUB
Receive all new releases from MSIA, except items specifically excluded. Soul Awareness Discourses and SAT subscriptions can be renewed automatically. Charges are billed to your credit card.

THE NEW DAY HERALD
MSIA's newspaper is an excellent resource for staying up to date with upcoming events, events sponsored by related organizations, products, photo and text reports on recent happenings. Every other issue features an article by John-Roger and John Morton. (Sent bi-monthly to each Discourse subscriber; also available through www.msia.org and www.ndh.org)

SOUL AWARENESS DISCOURSES
The heart of MSIA's teachings. (Twelve books per year, one for each month, English, Spanish, or French, #5000)

SOUL AWARENESS TAPE (SAT) SERIES
A new John-Roger seminar every month, plus access to the entire SAT library of hundreds of meditations and seminars. (Twelve tapes per year, one sent each month, #5400)

SOUL FLIGHT SERIES
Discourses for children. (Twelve discourses per year, one for each month, #5600)

VIDEO CLUB SERIES
A monthly John-Roger or John Morton video tape seminar which is preceded by a Moment of Peace video short from the Traveler's journeys around the world. (Twelve video tapes per year, one sent each month, #5800)

MSIA ON THE INTERNET
www.msia.org
The web site offers a free subscription to MSIA's daily inspirational e-mail, Loving Each Day; *The New Day Herald* on-line; the opportunity to request that names be placed on the prayer list; MSIA's catalog, and much more.

LOVING EACH DAY E-MAIL
Daily inspiration quotes from John-Roger and John Morton sent to your e-mail address. Free subscription is available in English, Spanish, French and Portuguese. Request Loving Each Day from www.msia.org.

ON LINE PTS CLASSES
Contact PTS for offerings and schedules.

MSIA INTERNET SITES

www.theblessings.org
www.forgive.org
www.lovingeachday.org
www.ndh.org
www.mandevillepress.org
www.msia.org
www.networkofwisdoms.org
www.pts.org
www.religionfreedom.org
www.seeding.org
www.spiritualwarrior.org
www.tithing.org

TAPES, BOOKS AND SUBSCRIPTIONS ARE AVAILABLE FROM:

MSIA®
P.O. Box 513935
Los Angeles, CA 90051-1935
323-737-4055 FAX 323-737-5680
soul@msia.org
www.msia.org

ABOUT JOHN-ROGER

A teacher and lecturer of international stature, with millions of books in print, John-Roger is a luminary in the lives of thousands of people. For over three decades, his wisdom, humor, common sense, and love have helped people to discover the Spirit within themselves and find health, peace, and prosperity.

With two co-authored books on the *New York Times* Best-Seller List to his credit, and more than three dozen spiritual and self-help books and audio albums, John-Roger is an extraordinary resource for a wide range of subjects. He is the founder of the nondenominational Church of the Movement of Spiritual Inner Awareness (MSIA) which focuses on Soul Transcendence; President of the Institute for Individual and World Peace; founder and Chancellor of the University of Santa Monica; and President of Peace Theological Seminary & College of Philosophy.

John-Roger has given over 5,000 seminars worldwide, many of which are televised nationally on his cable program, "That Which Is," through the Network of Wisdoms. He has been a featured guest on the "Roseanne Show," "Politically Incorrect," and CNN's "Larry King Live," and appears regularly on radio and television.

An educator and minister by profession, John-Roger continues to transform the lives of many, by educating them in the wisdom of the spiritual heart.

ABOUT JOHN MORTON

John Morton's life is dedicated to peace, and to assisting people in discovering the divinity within themselves. For John, these are not just lofty ideals with little reference in day-to-day life, but attainable goals with practical application for business, government and education, as well as individuals.

John has put these principles into practice as a licensed counselor, workshop facilitator and consultant. Since 1979 he has worked and traveled for a number of organizations which share his focus. These include: The Church of the Movement of Spiritual Inner Awareness, an ecumenical church that teaches practical spirituality where John has served as President and is currently the Spiritual Director; the Institute for Individual and World Peace, which fosters the study of peace as a "way of living without againstness"; the University of Santa Monica, which grants graduate degrees in counseling and spiritual psychology; and on the board of the New Visions Foundation which is establishing private schools which deliver high standards of education to students of diversity. In addition, John and his wife Laura Donnelley Morton established The Good Works Foundation in 1993, which, through philanthropy, is dedicated to supporting good works wherever they are found, particularly innovative educational and cultural charities.

An outstanding athlete in his youth, John continues his dedication to health and fitness. He has carried the Olympic Torch, completed marathons and enjoys regularly working out and running in the many locations his travels take him. His eight-year-old daughter and two-year-old son also keep him fit and on the move.

For more information, please contact:
The Movement of Spiritual Inner Awareness®
(MSIA®)
P.O. Box 513935
Los Angeles, CA 90051-1935
Phone (323) 737-4055
FAX (323) 737-5680
email: jrbooks@msia.org
www.msia.org